Original title:
The Sparkle of a Scarf

Copyright © 2025 Creative Arts Management OÜ
All rights reserved.

Author: Julian Montgomery
ISBN HARDBACK: 978-1-80586-001-3
ISBN PAPERBACK: 978-1-80586-473-8

Luminous Layers of Forgotten Tales

A twist and a twirl, what a sight!
Old tales wrapped in colors so bright.
Knots and fringes hold secrets unspun,
Whispers of laughter when day is done.

Around the neck, it flutters with glee,
Like a dance partner, wild and free.
Each fold a story, silly but true,
Chasing the gray skies with a vibrant hue.

Celestial Cloaks in a Moonlit Night

Under the stars, with fabric so bold,
Mismatched patterns that never grow old.
A flappy flap here, a twist over there,
Each flick of the cloth takes away despair.

Oh look at it shine, like a comet's flight,
Wrapping around me, feeling just right.
A caper of colors in the cool air,
Moonlit giggles float everywhere.

The Joyful Texture of Togetherness

Two friends bundled in fabric delight,
Spinning and laughing until it feels right.
Tangled up laughter, a knot or two,
Like a riddle that's silly, simple, and true.

We sway like the wind, playful and spry,
Tiny threads making connections, oh my!
Each ruffled edge brings a chuckle so bright,
Together in chaos, we dance through the night.

A Kiss of Color Against the Chill

A splash of red, then a pop of green,
Funky patterns, the quirkiest seen.
Against the cold, it shimmies and shakes,
What a good laugh when the frosty wind wakes.

Wrapped up tight, we prance down the lane,
A rainbow of chuckles, dismissing the rain.
With every flap, a cheer of delight,
Colors collide in a carnival night.

Whispers in Woven Threads

In a corner of the closet, lies,
A garment full of giggles and sighs.
It tickles necks and dances around,
Causing laughter to bubble and sound.

With every twist and every twirl,
It beckons with a playful swirl.
The more you wear, the more it grins,
Unraveling secrets of silly spins.

Glimmering Dreams in Silk

A glint catches eyes, oh what a sight,
Dreams shimmer and shimmer, all day and night.
Silk threads whisper tales of fun,
Turning dull moments to a joyful run.

Each fold like a giggle, free and wild,
Bringing out the laughter of every child.
With a swish and a swoosh, it steals the show,
Making you twirl, putting on a show.

Dances of Color in the Breeze

Colors collide in a vibrant spree,
They flutter and float, oh can't you see?
With a shimmy and shake, they come alive,
Creating a scene where chuckles thrive.

Sunlight winks on every hue,
Tickling noses as it breezes through.
If fabric could giggle, oh what a sound,
A parade of hues, joy unbound.

Tapestry of Radiance

A patchwork puzzle of shiny delight,
Each piece is a memory, a playful sight.
With a wink and a nod, it teases the day,
Wrapping your worries in a snug array.

When mischief calls, it dons a new face,
A costume of whimsy, a charming embrace.
Oh, the stories it tells with every knick,
In a playful dance, it does its trick.

A Whisper of Colors on My Shoulders

Bright hues wave like flags,
A fashion parade unfolds,
Tangled knots in my hair,
Adventures that never get old.

Swirling patterns like a dance,
Caught in a gust of wind,
Chased by a playful dog,
My mischief now begins!

Kaleidoscope of laughter,
I trip over my flair,
Each time I make a step,
My life feels like a fair.

A flick of color, a wink,
Textures tease and play hide,
With every twist and turn,
My style is my pride.

The Dance of Textiles in Twilight

Under the moon's glow, fabrics gleam,
I twirl and sway, lost in a dream,
With each funny twist, I may trip,
But there's no stopping this colorful flip.

Silken whispers surround me tight,
As I perform my best clumsy flight,
Snagging coffee cups, oh what a sight,
Who knew my outfit could cause such fright?

In shadows, polka dots shine bright,
Frayed edges laugh, I'll hold them tight,
Through mishaps and giggles, I wear my pride,
A fabric symphony, let's take a ride!

As I spin and glide, oh what a tease,
This wardrobe's a riddle, never at ease,
With every swish, I spread joy and cheer,
A dance of textiles brings laughter near!

Whispers of Woven Threads

A crafty stitch with a twist,
Threads gossip like busy bees,
Each patch tells a story,
Of laughter, quirks, and breeze.

Laughter weaves into the seams,
As I try to make a knot,
Tangled up in my own dreams,
Who knew fabric could be so hot?

Fabrics blend and colors speak,
Each layer a giggle, a peek,
In my world of yarn and cheer,
Every outfit's a playful streak.

From silly hats to capes so grand,
My textile menagerie is unplanned,
With each silly look, I can confide,
That life's just better with joy as my guide!

Glistening Fabric Dreams

Under stars, my fabric shimmers,
As I dance, the world just glimmers,
A creature of threads and spark,
In the night, I leave my mark.

Lace flips and sequins whirl,
Fashion's a playful twirl,
I might trip over my own feet,
But every fall just tastes sweet.

I wear colors like candy floss,
Daring in textures, I'm my own boss,
With tinsel and threads making waves,
I am the laughter that misbehaves!

Each fabric holds a silly scheme,
With every sparkle, I live my dream,
And through it all, I find my way,
In this wacky costume ballet!

Secrets Carried in the Fabric's Fold

In the corner, whispers hide,
We all know about their pride.
Twists and turns you cannot guess,
Secrets lie in every dress.

An old cat jumped, oh what a sight,
Chasing the threads, it took flight.
Daring moves, a swish and a swirl,
Fabric giggles as it starts to twirl.

Daring escapades of a lost sock,
It ventured out to share a joke.
Wrapped in patterns, a tale unfolds,
Who knew fabric could be so bold?

Polka dots and stripes in a race,
Each a character with a face.
Came the breeze, took them away,
Quirky comrades, now gone to play.

Mysteries Wrapped in Gentle Threads

Threads of laughter, soft and bright,
Entwined with joy, a cozy sight.
Underneath, a riddle snug,
What is it? All just a bug?

A frayed edge holds a secret tight,
Did a gnome stitch in pure delight?
Each knot a giggle, each fold a tease,
In the fabric, mischief's breeze.

A nameless patch with a wink,
Beneath the seams, what do you think?
Elusive jokes, a little shy,
Woven wonders make us laugh and cry.

As we wear, we bring to life,
Comedic tales of joy and strife.
With every turn, the plot unfolds,
Gathered in warmth, in fabric gold.

Rainbow Hues Against the Grey

In the corner stands my stash,
A riot of colors—what a crash!
Twisted reds, greens, and blues,
A fabric party with wacky views.

Caught in laughter, the threads align,
Each layer tells a joke in time.
Faded grey can't dampen cheer,
It's just a canvas for the dear.

Pants a'flying, shirts a'whirl,
Fashion faux pas give a twirl.
Mismatched pieces, oh what glee,
Rocking the runway, a sight to see!

As they flutter with every step,
A waltz of colors, not a rep.
Let the bland world sit and stare,
Our dance of hues, beyond compare.

Tender Emblems of Winter's Dance

In the cold, a fabric flares,
Burrs and laughter fill the air.
What once was grand, is now a knot,
Layered warmth may miss the spot.

Snowflakes gather, join the fun,
Tickling threads, oh what a run!
A tangled mess of yarn and cheer,
This winter dance brings mischief near.

A bow that slipped, a shove, a spin,
Threads of chaos where puns begin.
Woolly wonders, bright and bold,
Tales of giggles need to be told.

So grab your gear and take a chance,
Let's join the fabric's merry dance.
For in every stitch, a laugh's delight,
Winter's embrace brings pure light.

A Burst of Warmth on a Chilly Day

When winter winds play hide and seek,
A wrap of fabric gives a cheeky peek.
It sways and swirls, a joyful tease,
Wrapping hugs that bring you to your knees.

Fluffy fuzzies laughing as they hug,
Like well-behaved sheep in a snug rug.
The frosty air can't dampen the cheer,
With every twist, it brings good vibes near.

Colors popping like confetti in air,
Bringing giggles, forget your despair.
A playful dance around your neck,
Silly antics that leave warm flecks.

Oh, what a sight, this dazzling flair,
On a cold day, it's quite a rare pair.
With every chuckle, you'll feel less gray,
A burst of warmth on a chilly day.

Weaving Light into Warmth

In tangled threads, there lurks delight,
A happy weave that feels so right.
Each loop and twist, a secret plot,
To ensnare your heart, oh, why not?

They twirl like dancers, frilly and bright,
Turning mundane to sheer delight.
With every knot, a giggle in tow,
They whisper tales, oh, don't you know?

Colors clash and patterns collide,
A joyful chaos, a playful ride.
Turn and twirl, let laughter abound,
In each soft fold, happiness is found.

So wrap it tight, let the fun begin,
A snuggly embrace that makes you grin.
Weaving light into warmth today,
Tickling toes, come out to play!

Threads that Dance in Whispered Breezes

Oh, look at that scarf, a swirl so grand,
It tickles the nose, not quite planned.
Dancing forth, with every breeze,
It waves like a flag, begging you to tease.

Floating softly, a flurry of flair,
Chasing your laughter through the air.
Around you it wraps, a playful tease,
Onlookers chuckle, oh, such mischief it frees!

A waltz in the park, it loves the show,
With style so bold, it steals the glow.
Each gust a giggle, a twirl, and a dip,
Threads that dance like they've had one too many sips.

So when you're outside, let it shine bright,
Embrace the joy, hold onto the light.
For in every swirl, and every twist,
You'll find a dance you cannot resist.

Shimmering Touches of Home

A cozy layer, it cradles so tight,
In a world of chilly, it sparks pure delight.
With colors that shine like stars in the night,
It tells silly jokes to keep spirits light.

Each fiber a memory, wrapped around,
In this playful fabric, joy is found.
Tickling your neck like a friendly cat,
Whispering warmth in a chatty pat.

Home is this wrap, a soft embrace,
Laughing together, it finds its place.
When life feels frozen, it sways and sings,
Shimmering touches that love always brings.

A wink, a dance, a flamboyant show,
Life's little pleasures begin to grow.
In every fold, it remembers your name,
A treasure of comfort, a sparkly game.

Lively Patterns Against a Dull Sky

In a world so grey and bland,
Bright colors take a bold stand.
Stripes and dots, they dance and twirl,
A playful jaunt, a fabric whirl.

With every flick, they catch the eye,
As if to say, "Oh me, oh my!"
What's that draped across your neck?
A rainbowed feast, a cheerful wreck!

They laugh at clouds with every fold,
Whispering stories of warmth untold.
Is it a scarf or a party hat?
So many looks, let's try them all at that!

Oh, how they sway, these colors bright,
Turning heads left and right!
Who knew a wrap could bring such cheer?
In a dull sky, they're the spirit's spear!

Flowing Reflections of Warmth

A gentle swish, a playful glide,
Worn with swagger, there's nothing to hide.
A cozy hug, yet wild and free,
A twinkle bomb, just wait and see!

Caught in the breeze, a cheeky tease,
Giggling whispers blend with the trees.
"Oh look at me!" the fabric shouts,
Turning grumpy frowns into sprightly pouts.

In shades of sunshine or moonlight's embrace,
Every fold offers a silly face.
Strutting down streets with grace like a gazelle,
Turning all heads like a fabric spell.

It's not just warmth, it's a grand affair,
Who knew that cloth could bring such flair?
With every entrance, laughter ignites,
A flowing aura of joyful delights!

The Beauty of Threads Intertwined

In a tapestry of colors bright,
Threads join hands, what a sight!
Stitching laughter in every seam,
A patchwork quilt of silly dreams!

Twirling round like a whirling dervish,
Each twist and turn, a dash of flourish.
"Hey, don't trip!" my scarf will sing,
While pulling pranks like a playful spring.

Knots and loops dance like a fair,
In a banquet of fabric, none can compare.
This jigsaw puzzle, hugs and sighs,
Where every thread a giggle lies!

Artistry wrapped 'round your neck,
Spinning tales, what the heck!
With every sway, the world's a stage,
In this vibrant fluff, we disengage!

A Symphony of Texture and Light

A cascade of fabric, oh what a show,
With textures that shimmer and colors that glow.
Plays hide-and-seek with the sun's warm rays,
Creating laughter in whimsical ways.

Oh, the charm of a playful twist,
As every tassel has a dance to insist.
"Stride with pride!" the fringes proclaim,
In this quirky game, nothing's the same.

The fabric sings, it weaves through the air,
With each gentle flutter, it doesn't despair.
A melody of warmth and silly cheer,
Making even the grumpiest crack a beer!

So wrap it around, let your spirit soar,
In this symphony of joy, you'll crave for more.
A swirl of textures, a light-hearted fight,
Where every glance ignites pure delight!

A Canvas of Dreams on a Chilly Day

On the chilly breeze I wear,
A colorful thing with flair.
It dances wildly, what a sight,
It flutters like a kite in flight.

Neighbors stare and sometimes laugh,
As I balance like a giraffe.
Each twist and turn, a comic show,
Chasing warmth while looking so pro!

Winter's chill, my friend so bold,
With hues of blue and hints of gold.
A mixing palette on my neck,
My laughing scarf, a joy to deck.

So here I strut, a scarf so grand,
With every wave, I make a stand.
A canvas bright, a frosty day,
I wear my laughter, come what may.

Mosaics in the Wind

The wind blew strong, a playful tease,
My scarf went flapping like a breeze.
It flipped and flopped, a dizzy dance,
As I tried to catch it, what a chance!

Neighbors giggled, quite the sight,
As my scarf took off in flight.
A patchwork gone rogue, wild and free,
Who knew my scarf would act like me?

It wrapped a tree, then chased a bird,
A colorful blur, so absurd.
With every twist, it made me laugh,
Who'd think a scarf could cause such gaff?

In the end, we laughed and played,
My scarf and I, a grand parade.
Mosaics fluttering in the breeze,
A silly dance that aims to please.

The Journey of a Twinkling Thread

A twinkling thread upon my neck,
Just like a party, what the heck!
It trails behind, like a puppy's game,
It flirts and teases, what a fame!

As I walk, it pulls me back,
A comical chase, a silly track.
Every knot tells a tale untold,
Of laughter shared in the winter cold.

It wraps around, a spinning wheel,
With every twist, this joy I feel.
A journey bright, so full of cheer,
I lost the thread, oh dear, oh dear!

But back it came, with a wink and nod,
A merry prank, a little odd.
Through giggles and loops, it boldly led,
A twinkling thread, my lively thread.

Fragments of Magic in Every Loop

In every loop, a magic spun,
A scarf of colors, so much fun.
It tickles my neck, a playful sprite,
Lighting up the bland of night.

It twists and twirls, a joyful flick,
A fashion choice that does the trick.
With every wear, a laugh does bloom,
Who knew fashion could lighten gloom?

A hijinks fest in chilly air,
With this bright adornment, I dare.
A patchwork puzzle made with grace,
Each fragment shines, a happy face.

So here I stand, in layers bold,
A cushion of wit, a tale retold.
Fragments of cheer in a scarf's embrace,
Turning every moment into a race.

A Veil of Twinkling Hues

A colorful wrap, flung with glee,
It dances on shoulders, wild and free.
In a swirl of laughter, it twists and twirls,
A merry companion to all the girls.

Tickling the nose with a vibrant cheer,
It whispers secrets only friends can hear.
A quick flick here, a twirl just so,
And suddenly you're a star of the show.

Invisible giggles lace through the threads,
Silly poses strike, banishing dreads.
A fluttering friend in the brightest parade,
With it on, all worries just seem to fade.

Fashion faux pas? Never you mind,
It's chaos and charm in every unwind.
So wrap it around, give a spin or two,
A snug hug of colors that'll comfort you.

Threads of Light and Laughter

In a cupboard so deep, where the odd socks hide,
A treasure awaits, it's full of pride.
Tangled in laughter, each strand has a tale,
Worn by a buddy, old Dave, or a whale.

With a flick of the wrist, it takes on a life,
Waving away woes and adding some strife.
It flips like a pancake, rolls like a ball,
Draws circles of joy, while it giggles and falls.

So bring on the party, the silliness shines,
With threads of mirth and a splash of designs.
Each color a chuckle, each pattern a jest,
An outfit that guarantees you'll be dressed best.

Worn in the garden or on the town square,
It catches the sunlight and won't play it fair.
Laughter and whimsy? Oh yes, please apply!
For life's not complete without this cheeky high.

Shadows of Warmth in the Gloom

In a corner, it lies, with a shy little grin,
This fabric of fun, containing some sin.
When draped over shoulders, it keeps joke in tow,
Its cozy embrace makes shadows go slow.

The corners quiver with mischievous flair,
It makes sassy motions, beyond compare.
A cape or a blanket? It dares to be bold,
In moments of gloom, it breaks the mold.

"Why don't you wear me?" it jests with a wink,
It wraps around jokes as we all start to think.
Banishing dullness, replacing with zest,
In shadows we giggle, forget all the rest.

So if you feel glum in a monochrome maze,
Seek out this treasure, let colors amaze.
It swishes and sways, with glee in the room,
Lighting up spirits, chasing away gloom.

Embrace of Twilight Fabrics

In twilight's embrace, a fabric does lounge,
Waving goodnight in a mischievous scrounge.
It teases the cats with its colorful fling,
And whispers to stars as they start to sing.

"Just drape me with flair, let's star in a show,
I'll turn casual struts into a catwalk pro!"
With a flick of a wrist and a tap of the toes,
This charming companion encourages flows.

It tickles the senses with patterns bizarre,
Daring you to dance beneath the first star.
In twilight's soft glow, the silliness spreads,
And laughter erupts, filling up all the beds.

So gather the friends and come join the scene,
With warmth from the fabric, we'll reign like a queen.
In a whirl of delight and a gust of pure fun,
We'll strut through the night till the last day is done.

Radiant Veils of Winter's Breath

With colors bright like circus tents,
I tripped on silk as winter went.
A dance of yarn, a playful fling,
That scarf's a jester, hear it sing!

Wrapped around my neck so tight,
It tickles me, oh what a sight!
I start to twirl, I start to sway,
This fabric's got me, come what may!

With every twist, I lose a shoe,
A fashion faux pas, who ever knew?
It drapes like magic, flows like breeze,
I'm the star of giggles, if you please!

So here I am, in winter's cheer,
A scarf that laughs, let's give a cheer!
With patterns wild and colors loud,
I am the queen of scarfing proud!

Enchanting Wraps of Twilight's Glow

In twilight's gleam, I wrap and roll,
A charming chaos, what a goal!
It glimmers bright, a silly show,
I lost my hat, but here I go!

Each wrap a twist, a brand-new game,
My friends all laugh, I'm not to blame!
With shades of plum and royal blue,
It fluffs my ego, who need a crew?

I twirl around, it fluffs my head,
A windswept look, my neighbors dread!
They call me quirky, I just grin,
This scarf's a pal, we both win!

So here I prance, in jesting style,
With every knot, I steal a smile!
In laughter, warmth, and bright delights,
This wrap's a treasure and a fright!

Echoing Elegance in Every Stitch

Each woven thread a tale untold,
With polka dots and stripes so bold!
I strut in elegance, oh what a dream,
But here's the twist: I ripped a seam!

A giggle floats with every sway,
This crafted art will lead astray!
I pose in style, but watch my foot,
Tangled threads—a fashion hoot!

I turn to dance, I weave a patch,
The fabric laughs, it's quite the catch!
With playful grace, I skip and hop,
This scarf's a friend that won't let stop!

So if you see me strut with flair,
Just know this wrap is full of hair!
A bit of fun, a bit of flair,
In every stitch, there's love and care!

Shimmering Journeys of the Heart

Across the town, my scarf does zoom,
It flutters by like a silly plume!
In dazzling dance, it takes the lead,
I follow suit, I giggle in speed!

Adventure calls, it pulls me near,
Through puddles, leaves, and holiday cheer!
My neighbors wave, they cheer me on,
As the scarf drags—oh so long!

With every curl, my heart takes flight,
A laughing plume, oh what a sight!
A treasure trove of warmth and grace,
This fabric bond—my happy place!

So join the fun, grab your own flair,
And let it dance without a care!
For every stitch brings joy anew,
In sparkling threads, life's a zoo!

Polished Threads of Memory's Glow

In the closet, a chaos reigns,
Colors clash, oh what a pain!
A bright orange frill with polka dots,
Makes me ponder my fashion blots.

Once wore it at that awkward dance,
Tripped on it, lost my chance.
But laughter echoed through the hall,
As I staged my epic fall!

Useful for warmth, or so they say,
I'm still chilly in this flamboyant display.
Cousin Liz did call it chic,
But my fashion sense, oh so bleak!

Yet, in the end, it keeps me snug,
And tickles me like a playful hug.
With polished threads of joy's own glow,
I strut around like a fashion show!

Enveloping Whispers of Gentle Light

Wrapped up tight, it's quite a sight,
Hues that shimmer, oh what a delight!
I twirl and spin, like a whirling bee,
Neighbors question, 'Who could that be?'

Whispers of warmth in a chilly breeze,
Pulling off this look with quirky ease.
I strike a pose, the world's my stage,
As onlookers chuckle, I engage!

An accessory mishap, I can't ignore,
Caught in the door, it cries for war!
With a tug and a pull, this isn't quite cool,
A battle of fabric, no one plays the fool.

But laughing's the trick, so why not wear,
A tangled treasure that others may stare?
The gentle light wraps around my flair,
As I dance through life without a care!

A Tapestry of Hope and Warmth

Woven stories in every stitch,
Hopes and dreams, oh, quite the pitch!
Bright paisley swirls and stripes so bold,
My quirky shield against the cold!

At grandma's quilt, I snickered so,
Looks like a rainbow had a doughy throw!
Yet here I stand, a proud parade,
In this cozy chaos, I won't be swayed!

A fashion faux pas? Perhaps, just maybe,
But I'm the star of this silly spree!
Strutting on streets, with flair on show,
Leaving a trail of laughter aglow.

So join the dance and twirl around,
Life's too short to stand on the ground.
A tapestry bright, a sight to behold,
We wear our quirks, the hearts of the bold!

Glimmering Comfort on Cold Days

Frosty mornings call for flair,
Flashing colors, beyond compare!
In this knit that looks like a mess,
I feel like a queen in a cozy stress!

Neighbors peek through frosty panes,
Wondering who likes such bright gains.
I shrug and laugh, it's just my fate,
To be the jester of my wardrobe state!

A layered look, with joy on high,
As I strut in a pastel sky.
With a flip of fabric, I surprise the day,
Who knew my style led the way?

So here's to warmth that's funny and fun,
In this dazzling wrap, my day's just begun!
With comfort glowing, come what may,
I'll sashay forth, and smile all day!

Whirlwinds of Creativity in Fabric

A twirl, a twist, in the breeze it flies,
A vibrant whirl, it's no surprise.
With swirls of color, oh what a sight,
It dances and plays, a pure delight.

From grandma's attic, it calls my name,
A fabric treasure, never quite the same.
With patterns wild and prints galore,
Each stitch is magic, who could ask for more?

Around my neck, it finds its place,
It flutters and flops, with style and grace.
A takeoff moment, I spin and sway,
Who knew a cloth could steal the day?

In laughter we share, a smirk and a cheer,
This fabric wonder, bring humor near.
For in the fun of these patchwork runs,
Life becomes brighter, with fabric puns.

Enchanted Layers of Softness

A soft embrace, oh so divine,
Wrapped in layers, it feels just fine.
Each fold a secret, soft and sweet,
A cozy hug, oh, what a treat!

The first layer whispers, 'Just hold me tight,'
Another one giggles, 'Let's dance tonight!'
With every wrap, a chuckle ensues,
This softness brings joy, it's got the right hues.

Twisting and turning, it fights for the throne,
In a game of fashion, none feels alone.
With a flick of the wrist, it jumps to the floor,
A playful partner that leaves me wanting more.

Laughing out loud as it flutters and sways,
These layers of joy brighten dull days.
A whimsical charm in each fold and hue,
Who knew that fabric could giggle too?

Illumination in a Chilly Evening

As dusk wraps the world in a frosty embrace,
A flash of bright color joins the race.
It shines like a beacon, playful and bold,
A cheeky companion against winter's cold.

Beneath the stars, it flings and it flies,
A swirl of laughter beneath the skies.
In moonlight's glow, it catches the eye,
A merry fabric that loves to defy.

Tickling the cheeks of friends gathered near,
It wraps 'round our faces, igniting our cheer.
"This little number!" someone joyfully sings,
While chilly winds play with our warmth and flings.

In playful banter, we share our delight,
Each twirl brings a smile, a joyous sight.
So here's to the warmth and the spark that it gives,
In laughter and fun, together each lives.

The Artistry of Knots and Colors

With bows and twists, it comes alive,
A riot of hues where laughs can thrive.
Each knot tells a story, quite a vivid tale,
Of fabric adventures that never grow stale.

An artist at work with a playful design,
Colors entwined like a well-made vine.
Each loop and tangle brings giggles and glee,
A masterpiece formed, come dance with me!

In a whirlwind of fabric, we laugh and we play,
With knots and colors brightening the day.
The more that we tangle, the funnier it seems,
As we weave through this world, like running on dreams.

So here's to the laughter, the joy that it brings,
In every twist and every glimpse of spring.
For artistry flows where the colors unite,
In a tapestry woven, we share pure delight.

Enraptured in a Kaleidoscope of Threads

In a sea of vibrant hue,
My neck's a circus, it's true.
Twisting colors dance and play,
Like confetti on a sunny day.

Forest greens and fiery reds,
I look like I raided my threads.
Neighbors chuckle, what a sight!
A rainbow wrapped up tight.

With each turn, a giggle grows,
Laughter bursts with every pose.
Strangers pause, then join the fun,
In this tangled thread, we run!

So here I twirl on streets so wide,
In my silly yarny pride.
A walking joke, a playful whim,
Oh, what joy this scarf can brim!

Cozy Cahiers of Colorful Memories

Opening my closet door,
A treasure chest, I explore.
Each scarf a tale once told,
In colors bright, in weaves bold.

One scarf chases the winter blues,
Another flirts with autumn hues.
They giggle when it gets too warm,
Wandering out, they cause alarm.

Unruly knots and playful ties,
They bounce around, oh how they fly!
The fluff and fray, a jab and poke,
A wardrobe that just loves to joke!

Every time I don a piece,
I find a laugh, a moment's lease.
A cozy hug that can't be planned,
In laughter's weave, we hand in hand.

Illuminated Embraces of Fiber

Draped in golden threads so bright,
I dazzle like a disco light.
Neighbors stop and point in glee,
Did that scarf just wink at me?

As I strut down the sunny lane,
The sun reflects, but I feel no pain.
For each twirl, a giggle waits,
Creating smiles in funny states!

Woven fables of joy and love,
It sparkles brighter than a dove.
A toast to fiber, oh what cheer,
My giggling scarf, so full of cheer!

With every adornment, we take flight,
In a whirlwind of laughter, day or night.
Oh, this embrace of threads is grand,
My silly style, the best on hand!

Glinted Layers in a Frosty World

In frost's embrace, I waddle along,
My scarf sings a silly song.
Layers piled, I'm quite the sight,
Like a snowman in morning light.

Furry fluff and glimmering lace,
A fashionista's frosty face.
Sneaking peeks, birds freeze still,
They giggle at my winter thrill.

Every twist a canvas bold,
Stories of warmth told and retold.
Chasing snowflakes with fancy flair,
A scarf that dances, light as air!

So here I bounce in winter's chill,
With whimsy wrapped around my will.
Come share a chuckle, take a look,
At this glinting tale, a playful book!

Chasing the Fading Sunlight

I wrapped it tight, oh what a sight,
It danced and swirled in pure delight.
A vibrant flash caught in the breeze,
I chased it down with a giggling tease.

Around my neck, it flapped and flew,
Betrayed my charm, who knew it too?
A vibrant glow, it caught a bird,
And off it went, oh how absurd!

I spun it round, a joyous flair,
It whacked my friend—he gave a glare.
We laughed aloud as it took flight,
Waving goodbye with all its might.

Now as I sit and muse, oh dear,
It climbs the trees, like it has no fear.
A silly thing, yet full of fun,
Chasing laughter under the sun.

Crystals on a Wistful Whisper

With every twist, it glimmers bright,
A dainty charm in the fading light.
I whispered secrets into its fold,
But it laughed back, oh, so bold!

The neighbor's cat gave it a stare,
As it fluttered softly through the air.
I tried to catch it, quick as a wink,
It turned to me with a playful clink.

Glimmers danced where shadows lay,
A mischievous wink, it led me astray.
It snagged a twig, it tumbled down,
A sparkly crown on my head it found.

But now it lies with mischief stowed,
Wrapped in laughter, in stories flowed.
Who knew a cloth could bring such cheer?
A crystal dream, forever near.

Shimmering Stories in Every Fold

Every fold tells tales of cheer,
Woven moments, bright and clear.
I wrapped myself in shimmering tales,
As it wiggled out, oh how it fails!

A dashing sprint, it slipped away,
Caught on a branch, what a display!
I waved goodbye, it waved back too,
Our dance of fabric, just me and you.

With stories bold, and laughter high,
It caught the stray leaves in its sly.
Twisted around, it mockingly spun,
A jester's prank—a beautiful run!

Oh, how I twirl, with each bright story,
This fabric life, a funny glory.
In every crease, a laugh unfurls,
Shimmering tales of adventure swirls!

Echoes of Elegance in Twirls

In elegant loops, it twirled and swayed,
Brought out my clumsiness, oh the charade!
It led me on a wobbly trip,
A fashion statement that made me skip.

I danced like a fool in the curious park,
The squirrels laughed at my silly spark.
My scarf took flight, what a sight to behold,
An elegant waltz, a story retold.

Around the fountain, it happily spun,
Engaging pigeons in dazzling fun.
With every flap, I felt like a queen,
In my mismatched outfit, a fashion machine!

Now it sits, tired from the spree,
Whispers of laughter, a tune just for me.
An echo of elegance, and a bit of absurd,
In every twirl, the joy is interred!

A Bundle of Colors Against the Night

In twilight's embrace, colors collide,
A riot of hues on a joy-ride.
Wrap me in warmth, a wild, bright scheme,
Fashion doth whisper, a whimsical dream.

A tangle of threads, oh what a sight,
Dancing and twirling, pure delight.
Neighbors all gawk, with puzzling grins,
What's that on the fence? Oh, just my wins!

Swaying like tales told in jest,
Colors leaping, they never rest.
I trip on the hem, a comic affair,
Laughter erupts, hangs thick in the air.

A bundle of chaos, my lovely flair,
Drifting and twirling without a care.
In the realm of night, boastful and bright,
What fun to be wrapped in this playful light!

Dreamy Stitches of Celestial Comfort

Stitched by the stars, so soft, so sly,
I wear it with flair, oh my, oh my!
In colors so bold, a celestial scheme,
Futile attempts, they burst at the seams.

Misfits unite, with frayed, happy ends,
A cosmic blanket, where humor transcends.
Giggling threads, in a tangled embrace,
Wrap me in laughter, this zany space.

Onlookers chuckle, as I take a twirl,
Fashion faux pas? I give it a whirl.
With moonlight's glow, my outfit declared,
What a spectacle! They marvel, then stare.

Oh, dreamy stitches of silly delight,
Cuddling me close, both day and night.
Lie beneath the sky, those whimsical beams,
Wrapped in this laughter, chasing my dreams!

Textured Radiance on a Starlit Path

A swirl of textures, vibrant and bold,
Glinting under stars, a sight to behold.
I saunter along, where moonbeams collide,
Dripping with charm, like a joyful ride.

Each step is a joke, with flair in the night,
My cloak flares like fireworks, a comical sight.
Peering from shadows, "What's that?" they gasp,
Awakening wonder, in stitches they clasp.

It tickles the ground, a turbulent spree,
Whirling and twirling, just let it be!
With every lost thread, a giggle erupts,
This fabric of dreams, we're all so entrapped.

Toasting to laughter beneath velvet skies,
Texture and radiance - who would've thought?
Join in the dance, let the starlight play,
As joy weaves through shadows, come what may!

Cascades of Color in Nature's Cloak

Nature throws colors, what a wild spree,
Cascades of hues stretched out just for me.
Wearing this brilliance, like a peacock's strut,
Giggles abound, with each silly cut.

The wind plays tricks, it whispers and spins,
As I leap and tumble, oh where to begin?
Leaves join the party, they rustle with glee,
I'm just a marionette, oh let me be free!

With every misstep, chaotic delight,
I'm tangled in laughter, but feeling so light.
Nature's own canvas, I twirl and I spin,
Each splash of color, embracing my grin.

Cascades of joy as the day turns to night,
Draped in the charm that makes everything right.
So here's to the folly that colors our plight,
In nature's great cloak, let's dance till first light!

Vibrant Hues Against Gloom

In a closet, colors clash,
Bright yellows, reds, they flash.
Feeling blue? Just take a peek,
A rainbow hug, it's what you seek.

On gloomy days, I twirl around,
Stars of fabric, joy unbound.
My neighbors squint, they can't believe,
A walking party, watch me weave!

Amid the gray, these shades collide,
Flashing bright, I take my stride.
In polka dots, I'll lead the cheer,
Announcing spring will soon be here!

With every spin, a laughter burst,
These vibrant threads, they quench my thirst.
Who knew a scarf could spark such fun?
Let's dance and spin until we're done!

Dreamscapes Wrapped in Velvet

In velvet dreams, I stroll and glide,
With patterns swirling side to side.
A secret world within each fold,
Where magic tales and laughter unfold.

Jokes tumble out, like threads unwound,
In every stitch, a giggle found.
I'm a jester in a fabric trance,
Bumping into walls, watch me prance!

Each tassel wiggles, oh what a scene,
Misfits adore this vibrant sheen.
Tickled by whispers from cloth so fine,
I trip and tumble, just divine!

The hours fly, like threads on air,
In velvet glory, I've not a care.
With every wrap, I wear a grin,
In this cocoon, let the fun begin!

Tangles of Joy in a Winter's Breath

Snowflakes fall with chilly grace,
My scarf becomes a tangled lace.
Each twist and turn a chuckling sight,
A cozy mess, pure delight!

I duck and dive, 'neath playful flakes,
Watch out, a winter jest awaits!
My scarf unwinds, a kite in flight,
Chasing snowmen, oh what a plight!

A muffled giggle, can't be stopped,
As every knot, my joy has dropped.
In frozen fields, I dance and twirl,
A whirlwind of warmth in a frosty swirl!

With every twiddle, laughter soars,
This scarf's my hug, forever yours.
In winter's breath, we find our cheer,
Each jumbled thread a reason to cheer!

Cascades of Warmth and Wonder

From edges frayed, imagination flows,
A cascade of warmth in vibrant shows.
Flapping corners, a whimsical flight,
As I prance about, a comical sight!

Each hug I give, a laughter spree,
Wrapped in joy, it's plain to see.
With every loop, a playful tease,
My mismatched patterns aim to please!

Around my neck, oh what a twist,
A merry dance you can't resist.
With every turn, the giggles bloom,
Creating cheer that fills the room!

And when I trip, a bundle of fun,
Surrounded by warmth, my joy has spun.
In cascades bright, we find our grace,
A tapestry of laughter, woven in place!

Woven Dreams in the Frosty Air

In a pile of threads bright and bold,
Lies a tale that must be told.
Wrapped around a frozen neck,
It's a fashion choice, what the heck!

Swirling patterns dance with glee,
Like a wild child in a tree.
Knots and loops that tease the eye,
While keeping warmth, oh my, oh my!

Colors clash like birds in flight,
A vibrant scene, what a sight!
Flailing flaps like a flag on high,
Watch it blow, just give it a try!

So grab that fabric, don't delay,
It's a cozy, funny, warm ballet.
Laugh with friends in chilly air,
As you flaunt your scarf with flair!

Captivating Shadows in Cozy Corners

In shadows cast, the laughter fades,
But not with threads that never age.
Artsy knots, a crafty play,
Making fashion statements each day.

A cozy nook, a scarf awry,
Who knew it could fly so high?
Tangled tails that twirl and swirl,
A whirlwind dance, oh what a whirl!

Hiding secrets of warmth and style,
With a wink and a quirky smile.
Every twist whispers tales of cheer,
In the corners we hold so dear.

So let it dangle, let it sway,
In cozy corners let it play.
When shadows stretch, just have a laugh,
With your silly, tangled scarf graph!

Trails of Twinkling Threads

On a snowy path, with style, we strut,
Trailing behind, a colorful glut.
Twinkling threads in a jolly race,
Chasing giggles with every trace.

A rainbow ribbon on winter's breeze,
Tickling noses, bringing ease.
Each bob and weave a funny jest,
As it wraps us up, we're feeling blessed!

Giggling while we play in snow,
An ensemble of fun, don't you know?
As slip and slide, we tumble and roll,
Our jolly trails take a toll!

So let them trail, the threads so bright,
In every bobble, pure delight.
In playful chaos, we find our way,
With twinkling trails, let's seize the day!

Vibrant Embrace of a Winter's Day

A frosty morn, the world out glows,
Draped in colors that no one knows.
Every wrap brings a chuckle and cheer,
In vibrant embrace, winter draws near.

Puffy and warm, it sways with style,
Drawing smiles, it travels a mile.
Fluffy knots like a quirky beast,
In this warm hug, we feast!

Off to the market, scarves on display,
Watch them dance in a playful ballet.
Snickering at bumps, oh, what a sight,
Waving our arms, feeling so light!

So twist and twirl; it's all for fun,
In this vibrant world, we've truly won.
With every layer that snugs so tight,
Let's savor winter, oh what a delight!

Echoes of Color and Warmth

In the corner, a riot of hues,
My scarf's a joker, spreading good news.
Twisted like a pretzel, a fashion delight,
It tickles my nose, oh what a sight!

Swirling like confetti, it catches the breeze,
With every loud laugh, it aims to please.
A dance with the wind, it twirls so proud,
I'm dressed like a clown, in front of the crowd!

Covering my face in a silly disguise,
Can't tell if it's me or those bright butterflies.
Onlookers giggle, in joy they unite,
Fashion's no serious business, that's right!

So here's to my garment, a bundle of joy,
A rainbow in fluff, my playful decoy.
A tangle of threads, oh what a thrill,
Wear it with laughter and a warm, happy chill!

A Dance of Yarns in the Light

A waltz on my shoulders, a twist and a twirl,
My colorful wrap makes me spin, jump, and whirl.
Laughter around me ignites like a flame,
In this game of fabric, I'm crazy, not tame!

A pirouette here, a dip and a slide,
Frolicking freely, full of bright pride.
Oh, the colors collide, what a frantic ballet,
This whimsical dance steals the breath away!

With each silly pose, I strike a new stance,
Creating a theorem of yarns in a dance.
My scarf's an accomplice, a partner in cheer,
We weave through the crowd, both sparkling and clear!

So here's to the yarns that glitter and play,
In the spotlight, they shimmer, oh what a display.
No fabric quite like it, with mischief it's fraught,
A lighthearted journey, oh what fun we've caught!

Threads of Joy in a Gentle Breeze

A burst of bright colors, my scarf's in the sun,
With laughter and breezes, it's pure, silly fun.
Tickling my neck, what a light-hearted tease,
A fluttering friend, in the dance of the leaves!

With my own personal jester that knots and spins,
It whispers sweet secrets, cheeky little grins.
Each sway and each wiggle tells tales in the air,
Of warmth and of friendship that's playful and rare!

Like a kite in the wind, it flops and it flies,
Though tangled and knotted, it never complies.
Making new mischief wherever I roam,
This burst of delight feels just like home!

So here's to the threads of joy held so tight,
Woven in laughter, they shine oh so bright.
Under the sun, we share all our woes,
A friendship like this, it brilliantly glows!

Chasing Sunshine with Every Fold

In folds and in creases, my scarf sings along,
With every bright pattern, it's calling a song.
Chasing the sunlight, it bounces with glee,
A happy companion, just like you and me!

Tangled in giggles and soft little frills,
It dances through markets, over sharp hills.
Oh, a flap here and there, with vibrant delight,
This playful companion loves daylight so bright!

Like a puppy that leaps just to see the blue sky,
It pulls on my heartstrings like a swift butterfly.
A chase through the park, laughing, wild, and bold,
Together we wander, with stories untold!

So here's to the joy in each playful fold,
A trove of bright colors and memories old.
With laughter in tow, let's frolic, let's play,
For chasing the sunshine makes every day gay!

The Charm of a Fluttering Embrace

A twist of fabric, bright and bold,
It tickles my nose, just like I've told.
It wraps around me, with playful glee,
A mischievous partner, as wild as can be.

It flaps in the breeze, a whimsical dance,
Like a wily bird, in a clumsy prance.
A game of tug, with a stubborn cat,
No more dignified, I surrender to that!

Each flick and flutter, makes me laugh loud,
As it loops and tangles—oh, what a crowd!
I'm wearing a rainbow, or a circus tent,
Who knew a piece of cloth could have such intent?

Flaunting its flair, with a whimsical twist,
Caught in the chaos, I surely insist.
This fluttering garment, it needs its own show,
With giggles and chuckles, we steal the tableau.

Silken Secrets Beneath the Moon

Beneath the night sky, twinkling and bright,
A silky secret takes flight in the night.
It glimmers and glows, like stars in the dark,
Tied to my waist with a dramatic spark.

It hides my dinner, a mischievous plot,
In every fold, remnants of what I've got.
Oh fruity jam stains, like badges I wear,
An honored display of my culinary flair!

This fabric's a joker, can't sit still for long,
It flutters and flaps, like a karaoke song.
A fabric-induced dance party, just for me,
Waltzing with shadows, oh who could foresee?

Now I prance like a peacock with tales to share,
The moon chuckles softly, as I lose my hair.
So here's to the night, my secrets held fast,
A silken companion, present and past.

A Symphony of Color and Comfort

In hues of joy, it wraps me tight,
A symphony plays, like pure delight.
Colors collide, a playful parade,
Even a frown, it can't evade!

A polka-dot twirl, a jazzy flip,
It lifts my spirits, gives my stride a lift.
With each gentle twist, I break into song,
Frolicking freely, nothing feels wrong.

The patterns collide, with gusto galore,
I'm wearing a party, who could ask for more?
A concert of fabric, it dances in time,
Announcing my presence, in rhythm and rhyme.

So let the colors sing, let the fun begin,
With laughter and joy, let the giggles spin.
A whimsical cloak, where comfort's a must,
In the spirit of fun, this fabric I trust.

Threads of Joy in Winter's Grasp

In winter's chill, I bundle in bliss,
With threads of joy that I can't resist.
Like a marshmallow puff in a snowball fight,
I tumble and fumble, what a silly sight!

It wraps around me, a snug little hug,
A cozy delight, like a warm, friendly rug.
But wait! What's this? A spill on my sleeve!
Eggnog's gone rogue, what a crafty reprieve!

Dashing through flakes, I frolic and run,
With each merry twist, I'm just having fun.
It tickles my chin, as I giggle and grin,
A swirling adventure, let the chaos begin!

So here in the frost, I dance with delight,
In threads of joy, that twinkle so bright.
With laughter and warmth, I embrace the snow,
In this silly attire, my joy will just grow!

Lush Colors in a Canvas of Frost

In winter's chill, a rainbow blooms,
Colors dance in vibrant flumes.
A silly scarf around my neck,
Keeps my warmth, what the heck!

It swirls and twirls with every stride,
Causing laughter far and wide.
Neighbors gawk at my fashion sense,
I just grin, immense suspense!

It catches snowflakes, a frosty feast,
Looking like a festive beast.
With reds and greens, it steals the show,
A jolly sight, don't you know?

Oh, how it jingles when I twirl,
Making winter feel like a whirl.
In this canvas of frost and cheer,
Who knew a scarf could bring such gear?

Fragments of Light

In the gray of winter's gloom,
Comes a scarf that dares to bloom.
It sparkles like a disco ball,
Making snowy days enthrall!

Neighbors peer from their windows,
Is it art or just a joke that glows?
With every move, it shines so bright,
Turning heads left and right!

Yet tangled in a gusty breeze,
It flutters like a teasing tease.
Twirling around like a playful sprite,
Chasing my shadow in pure delight!

Oh, the joy of this colorful find,
Leaves me laughing, never blind.
When wearing this, how could I fret?
My wardrobe's best, you can bet!

Stitch by Stitch

Knitted threads in hues so bold,
A story of warmth, yet to be told.
I donned it with pride on a frosty morn,
Suddenly, I was fashion's unicorn!

Each loop and twist, a vibrant rhyme,
I strut like a peacock, it's party time!
With stitches bright, it steals the scene,
Fuzzy laughter bursts between!

Once it snagged a passing dog,
We twirled together in winter's fog.
It dragged him across the fluffed white street,
Who knew fashion could be so sweet?

So here's to the love of threads and seams,
Dancing through life with wild dreams.
In stitches, fun is surely rich,
Wear it proudly, stitch by stitch!

Serendipitous Colors in a Gentle Wind

A playful breeze swept through the town,
And here I was, in colors profound.
My scarf, a whirlwind of joy and light,
Turns the mundane to pure delight!

Flapping wildly like a giant bird,
Each flutter leaving little disturbed.
People chuckle, their faces aglow,
As I prance with my rainbow show!

The wind whispers secrets of what may come,
While I act like the silliest bum.
Swirls of joy twist around me,
Who knew winter could dance so free?

In serendipity lies the thrill,
This scarf of mine brings laughter and chill.
I'll twirl and spin, make no mistake,
For joy is what I choose to create!

Enchanted Textures of a Winter's Tale

A winter's tale unravels with flair,
As my scarf swirls in the crisp air.
The textures tell stories, oh what a sight,
Creating giggles, pure delight!

It's plaid, it's polka, it's stars and stripes,
Bouncing around like little gripes.
Each layer wraps me in serendipity,
Funny faces wear the epitome!

Caught in a gust, oh what a dance!
This scarf leads me straight to chance.
With every twist, a new mishap,
Who knew winter could make me clap?

So here I twirl, in this cozy land,
With laughter spilling like grains of sand.
In enchanted textures and gleeful trails,
I'll wear my joy, no one fails!

www.ingramcontent.com/pod-product-compliance
Lightning Source LLC
Chambersburg PA
CBHW060146230426
43661CB00003B/587